Disparity

There are many people who

Lonely like a bre___ __

But that loneliness is enough to hurt any man

For he stays away from the fish in the sea

He learns to bottle up his feelings

Like a prison door, he is sealed up tight

And a prison, his life has become

Outsiders are merely visitors

He learns to find reasons not to open up his prison doors

As in all cases, his loneliness gets to be too much

He then tries to leave this prison of his life

The only way he thinks he can

His attempt will take him from the world of the living

He goes for it but forgets about the visitor of his prison

The visitor stops him and sits him down

She tells him that his life is so important

That he shouldn't end his physical form

She wants him to not feel alone

His prison, she wants him to leave behind

She wants him to live a normal and social life

In the end, he has abandoned his prison

That prison is now forgotten in history to never be opened again

Thanks to that visitor, he is still alive and happy to this day

Don't give up like he wanted to

Life is important

Live it

Difference

People have a fear of difference

Whether they got the habit from family or friends, we will never know

They do not like difference, for change is likely to follow

Many people do not like change, which drives the fear of difference

The more people do not like change, the harder it will be to embrace change

All it takes is one person for change to be embraced

The fear of change can be taken away

We are all different in our own ways

Some are born with a difference

Others are different to be the best they can be

That fear of difference needs to be locked away

So far away that the fear is long forgotten

Change needs to come

But to have change, difference is needed

Embrace the difference

Change is surely to follow

Or be the change

And make a difference

A change is going to come

The Princess You Are

There are many princesses in this world

I know you are a princess

The fairest of them all

The most special of them all

This kingdom of yours is amazing

Fit for a princess

And a princess

One day you will find your prince

Together you can rule your kingdom

And he would be the luckiest man in the world

For having such an amazing princess like you

Two Face

There are many people who have been through a lot

Some, their entire lives

They only choose to hide their feelings

Out in public, they are one person

In their private life, who they are

Many people do not know about the person's life

As it is not shown in public

Over time, it is perfected so they seem more natural

As the new person they have become

The longer they stay as the person, the worse they will get

Their private person will start to fade away

Leaving the new person living as he is more accepted

It sinks them deeper into the deep darkness

People never knew the real him

Then he began having unusual behavioral patterns

One person asks if they are okay

The person helps them until their old self comes back

Do not be afraid to show your true self

You do not need to be who you are not just to be accepted

Embrace the real you

Meaning of Life

People question the meaning of life

Others question their purpose

Many have yet to think about it

You don't have to know your purpose from the day of puberty

Everyone has a purpose

There is a meaning to life, despite your size, height, or weight

You will discover your purpose

It might be in high school or in your career

I believe your purpose is amazing as you are as a person

I have questioned my purpose in life many times

My purpose was also being questioned

For that was the biggest mystery

But do not be frustrated

You will find your purpose

And you will find the meaning of life

Music of the Voice

Many people have the voice as soft as a gentle breeze

Many people have the voice as bad as nails on a chalk board

I for one did not have a good voice

People with amazing singing voices never share

Their talent never being known

The people with the worst voices sing out

Eventually getting better over time

Everyone wishes they can sing

They can be an amazing singer

The first place to start success is with yourself

Many people can already sing

Whether born with the talent,

Or going through countless lessons

Anyone can do it

For every new singer comes a unique style of music

As no one has the same voice or style

That is why there is a variety

So you might have a voice like a nail on a chalk board

But over time, with practice

It can be as soothing as the waves crashing upon the sand

Do not be afraid to show off

For one day, greatness is sure to follow

Mighty Kingdom of Yours

Out of all the kingdoms in this world

I have never found one as mighty

None are as mighty as yours

Out of all the princesses in this world

None are like you,

You are the best of all the kingdoms

A kingdom we will one day rule

You are like a pure angel

That sure is not a lie

Your voice is as calming as a gentle breeze

You are everything that cannot be replaced

This kingdom we will one day rule

Hospital Visit

Be careful how you treat people

You never know what that person went through

Their parents could be divorcing and have to choose to be with one parent

They could be bullied and harassed for so long

Or they could be abused at home

All it takes is one little push in the wrong direction

And the person will try to come up with a way to end their selves

I for one was pushed past that point

Thoughts were going through my mind left and right

People noticed I wasn't thinking right

I was brought before my teacher and sent to the ER

Then transferred to a behavioral health hospital

There I stayed a week and a half

Talking about how I felt and given an antidepressant

Since that trip, my life has changed

I see my life in a new light

My life changed for the better

If you know someone is going through things

Take some time out of your life

Sit and talk to them

You could save a life

Our Men in Blue

Many of our police go unappreciated now a day

They do so much to protect us and keep us safe

If it was not for them being in that job

Crime rates would be much worse than they are now

They put their lives on the line every day

I told a police officer, Lawrence Howell, that I appreciated him

After I told him that, he had a big smile

He told me that he rarely hears that

We need to let them know that they are appreciated

Give them a gift or just tell them in person

They are humans too

Who want to know they are appreciated

And to be told that they are wanted

We will always need them

As they are the law and protector of people

Give them appreciation

You could make their day

Back to Vietnam

Vietnam veterans came home to a rude welcoming

They were spit at, called names, cursed, and not welcomed

Some of them had willingly joined the service

Others were drafted against their will

The ones who avoided were imprisoned

Some enlist into another branch to avoid the draft

They fight in Vietnam because they had not choice

Doing as they are ordered was what they had to do

Their friends, they watch die in front of them

They had to do horrible things because of their orders

The wives of the veterans were treated like their husbands

Vietnam veterans have aged as unwelcomed soldiers

But they served our country and did as they were told

They served for us so that we can have today

But many gave up their tomorrows in Vietnam

So if you see a Vietnam veteran

Tell them, 'Thank you"

They will appreciate it and you might have a nice talk

Give them thanks as they really need it

My Heart Beat

Every time I talk to you

My heart beats

Like a clap of hands?

I think not

Like a clap of thunder?

I think not

My heart beats like a drum

It beats for you

My heart yearns for you

Like you are my true love

There are many girls in the world

Who would love to have me as theirs

But those women cannot have me

As I belong to only one woman

The woman who means so much to me

The woman is my everything

That woman is you

Whom I belong to

The Attempt Part 1

There are a few of you who will not believe this story

But this story is true

As it is a story about me

I have been "different" my whole life

People did not like that I was different

And I was bullied and harassed my entire life

Since elementary school, I put on a mask

Over the years, I learned how to improve it

So that people could like me

I was plunged into a deep depression

There seemed to be no end in sight

It seemed like I was alone

Like I was not wanted at all

Then came seventh grade

They noticed that I liked In School Suspension

So they had me tested for autism

Afterwards, I was diagnosed with High Functioning Autism

I felt it was the end of the world

There were three attempts of suicide

Over the span of three days

My mother walked in on all three

And stopped me

The Attempt Part 2

So I was given a mental health councilor

I have spent years talking to that person

And I was still bullied and harassed

That mask was so perfect that no one knew

All the stuff I have been through

I had a severe case of depression

And no one knew I had it and still do

The word happiness had no meaning to me

For I have not been happy for years

I had very bad trust issues

As I trusted no one, not even family

Paranoia was also developing in me

I prefer to be alone as I do not like crowds

Then I was jumped walking home from school my junior year

January of 2019, I attempted suicide for my fourth time

No one was home but I felt a hand placed on me

That caused me to stop my attempt

February of 2019, I was having suicidal thoughts

I was sent to Hill Crest Behavioral Health Hospital

There I stayed for a week and a half

Since then, my life has changed for the better

Please do not go through what I did

You are worth it

The Key to My Heart

You are on my mind every day

You have stolen my heart

I know you will not break it

You are my love, my life, my world

Forever keep me near

For in your arms, I am home

You have brought light into my once dark life

You showed me how to love

And love me like no other could

You make me the person I am

I am forever yours as you are mine

You are my pride and joy

I never want to lose you

So I will tell you once again

I love you oh so much

The Beginning

You might be wondering how I got into poetry

I was not a poet over night

My poetry used to begin with giving copied love poems

To my girl they would go

After many months of that, I began writing my own

So love poems were my start

I tried the many poetry styles and did not like them

Then I tried free verse

So I wrote free verse love poems for my lover

Then I wanted to branch from love poems

Each poem would have less love stuff in them

As I wrote poems about other things

But I went back to love poems

And I sent my girlfriend more love poems

My first non-love related poem was "Disparity of Life"

You may not be born with the gift

Just keep doing it

And do not give up

You are very talented

Leave all your options open

You can do it

Learning in School

People question whether we should go to school

A majority of people do not want to go

It is hard to tune them out

People who do not care make it hard for others to learn

Learning is a right for all

The ones who do not want to learn takes that right away

Which really makes people mad

I for one was aggravated at the people who do not care

But we have to put up with them

From elementary to high school

All we can do is try to learn

So they affect your grades

Without them, your grades would improve significantly

But we all cannot get what we want

If you are one who disrupts class

Please do not, for others may want to learn

Be respectful to others

Faith

People have the right to freedom of religion

Some take it so harsh and are straying from the words

They judge people who do not follow the same beliefs

But all men and women have equal rights

People should not be judged on their beliefs

Just knowing their faith does not mean you know the person

Take some time to get to know the person

Everyone is amazing in their own way

Whatever they believe, let them believe in it

And you believe in what you want

Faith is beautiful like a red rose

Like a rose it will grow

So cherish your religion

And the religion of others

Destruction of the Earth

We as human beings have been destroying our planet

Every year, at least one animal species goes extinct

Our everyday habits are destroying homes of animals

It is destroying our planet as we speak

The ozone layer is fading away

Leaving us open for solar radiation

The radiation is stopped by the ozone

We pollute our waterways with trash

Our trash is destroying ecosystems

It is also destroying good vacation spots

Even the air around us is polluted

Factories that spring up, constantly polluting the Earth

Cars, the best and fastest form of transportation

With every use, they release more pollutants

Trains, cars, planes, and boats

All release pollutants on to our planet

Pollution affects Earth more than you will ever know

We as people need to find ways to cut pollution down

Clean our waterways to help ecosystems

Possibly help solve a lot of the water crisis

Recycle and reuse a lot of our trash

Start using a bicycle more than your vehicles

There is so much we can do to help our planet

Let us help Earth Heal

Go green

You Are

You are the sunshine

That shines brightly throughout my life

You are the gravity

That holds me down in every way

You are the moon

That shimmers throughout my night

You are the stars that glimmer oh so bright

You are the oxygen that keeps me alive

You are the heart that beats inside of me

You are the blood that flows through me

You are the only woman I can see

You have the voice as a gentle rain shower

You are my everything

My one and only

You stop me from being lonely

To Our Military

Some people would say that we do not need a military

But in reality, we do

They allow us to sleep at home

Not having to worry every day

So we can live our everyday lives

They are our guardians

The ones who have sworn to protect us

Many men and women sign up

To their country they swear to protect

Their one thing, to keep us a free nation

Lives, they put on the line for us

We are worth it to them

They serve so we do not have to

Our duty as a nation is to honor them

They give up a lot of their rights for us

Show thanks to our service members

Past and present

They do so much

Disabilities

People are afraid of others with disabilities

They come up with crazy stories how the disability came

It makes people with the disability hate themselves

Disabilities are nothing more than an awesome superpower

People with disabilities tend to be talented

They are unique in their own way

Equality should be for all

Disability or not

Everyone is special in their own way

People with disabilities are amazing

They are very unique

Disabilities, they do not let stop them

True warriors, for all that they go through

Battles they have and will continue to win

Amazing people they are

Brave, smart, responsible, sweet

All characteristics that make them special

And what relates you to them

Please treat everyone equal

Disability or not

They are people too

Beauty of Nature

Such a beautiful word

For nature is everything

Technology can never replace it

Or replicate it

Technology has driven us away from nature

But true beauty lies outside our homes

Nothing can replace it

Exploration is natural to us

There is an endless world to explore

So much of it would be in nature

Nature is everything and is beautiful

But nature is dying

We are rising the demand for wood

So deforestation is constantly occurring

We have not done anything to stop the harm

We need to preserve the beauty of nature

So we can continue to explore her beauty

Lets be the change in our world

And bring back nature's beauty

Beautiful Rose

Nothing is prettier than a rose

A rose that shows its true colors

Roses are a beautiful wonder

The rise of the sun, I would not miss

For I know my rose is watching too

No other flower I could look at

As my rose has captured me

No other can have me

For only one rose deserves me

She is unique and special

That rose is like no other

A rose that is better than the sunrise

Beauty that is beyond compare

My rose I'd rather watch

Than the sunrise

For my rose deserves my attention

My rose she will forever be

Beauty Within

Lots of girls do not think they are beautiful

They would do anything to be beautiful

Some would starve themselves

Others would go through several surgeries

All because of the people of society

Society made "standards" or a woman

Standards for a woman should go away

Women are amazing just the way they are

They do not need to change themselves

To be who they are not

A person does not have to change to be accepted

People need not love them for who they are

Woman are unique and amazing

There is nothing about a woman to change

Do not love a woman for their outside beauty

Love them for the beauty within

The beauty within is all that matters

And to our women

Do not hate yourself for who you are not

Love yourself for who you are

You all are amazing just the way you are

The World of Languages

Languages are complicated

It is different from place to place

To learn a new language is hard

Complicated, it will always seem

As each is structured differently

It is harder to understand

How a word is spelled in one language

Is pronounced differently in another

Languages are one thing to make us unique

Some struggle to understand a new language

Others might tell you that your language is hard

English is actually one of the hardest languages

As it is very complex

Do not fear someone with a different language

Help them learn or cope with them

Struggles of Men

Men live a tough life

Society has set guidelines for a "real man"

They want men to be emotionless as a rock

Muscular, they also have to be

So they cannot be who they are

Or they will be looked down upon

They are fed the "guidelines" of society

It causes a lot of problems

Men are bullied if they do not follow these "guidelines"

Depression runs really high for them

People only think that it is only women with this problem

But that is where they are wrong

Men and women struggle with society

But we need to accept men for who they are

Not for who they are not

Let them live how they want to

They are perfect just the way they are

Unique, they should be allowed to be

We are all perfect for who we are

Do not follow false guidelines

Be who you are

And live your life

The way you want to live it

Only Time Will Tell

When I first met you,

I felt like I had known you forever,

Telling you my secrets

And what I did not want ever

You listened to me

I bet you thought I would never end

Who would have thought

That we would become more than just friends

Over a period of time

I got to know you

A woman so caring and gentle

With a heart so true

I told you I would never leave

Because of the feelings I have inside

And sometimes I wonder

What would I do if you were gone

So I have decided

Time answers all

If it is meant to be,

Time will remove the wall

You can always make me smile

Will it ever really be forever

Time will reveal what lies ahead

Thinking of You

As each star comes out to shine

As the wind rustles across the land

As the moonlight sweeps across the room

I am thinking of you

When the sun burns its morning greeting

When the birds chirp and swoop through the sky

When the leaves of trees dance through the air

I am thinking of you

During the haze of the afternoon sun

During the smooth swirl and flow across the sky

During the fade of the bustling day

I am thinking of you

When the twilight shadows begin to fall

While the evening air begins to chill

While the crickets begin their sweet evening chorus

I am thinking of you

Just as the darkest hour of the night falls

Just as the world is hushed and silent

Just as dreamland beckons

I am thinking of you

Every day

Every hour

Every moment

I am thinking of you

Made in the USA
Columbia, SC
29 July 2023

21018898R00017